Piano Music Theory

Swiftly Learn The Piano & Music Theory Essentials and Save Big on Months of Private Lessons! Chords, Intervals, Scales, Songwriting & More.

Tommy Swindali

© Copyright 2020 - All rights reserved.

The content contained within this book may not be reproduced, duplicated or transmitted without direct written permission from the author or the publisher.

Under no circumstances will any blame or legal responsibility be held against the publisher, or author, for any damages, reparation, or monetary loss due to the information contained within this book, either directly or indirectly.

Legal Notice:

This book is copyright protected. It is only for personal use. You cannot amend, distribute, sell, use, quote or paraphrase any part, or the content within this book, without the consent of the author or publisher.

Disclaimer Notice:

Please note the information contained within this document is for educational and entertainment purposes only. All effort has been executed to present accurate, up to date, reliable, complete information. No warranties of any kind are declared or implied. Readers acknowledge that the author is not engaged in the rendering of legal, financial, medical or professional advice. The content within this book has been derived from various sources. Please consult a licensed professional before attempting any techniques outlined in this book.

By reading this document, the reader agrees that under no circumstances is the author responsible for any losses, direct or indirect, that are incurred as a result of the use of the information contained within this document, including, but not limited to, errors, omissions, or inaccuracies.

Discover "How to Find Your Sound"

http://musicprod.ontrapages.com/

Swindali music coaching/Skype lessons.

Email djswindali@gmail.com for info and pricing

Table of Contents

Introduction
Chapter 1: Music Theory Fundamentals
Chapter 2: Scales, Modes and Keys
- The Difference Between Major And Minor Scales
    - The Major Scale
    - The Minor Scale
    - The Chromatic Scale
- Modes
    - Ionian Mode
    - Dorian Mode
    - Phrygian Mode
    - Lydian Mode
    - Mixolydian Mode
    - Aeolian Mode
    - Locrian Mode
- Keys

Chapter 3: Chords, Rhythms, And Movement In Music
- Chords
- Rhythm
- Movement in Music

Chapter 4: Songwriting
Chapter 5: Orders and Circles
Conclusion

References

Introduction

When making the decision to start learning to play music, specifically that of the piano and/or keyboard, we tend to not know where the best point is to begin. We may be told that YouTube videos are the best place to begin, or that books provide more detail. However, books are too text-heavy, with not enough visual images and diagrams. We tend to forget that many people are visual learners, leading to a quicker learning process when diagrams are included. Music books that are text-heavy are too complex for beginners, as well as being too mundane for the experienced. They lack the presence of lesson plans, which hold a novice musician accountable for their progress. Often, explanations are not included in text-heavy books, leading to a bout of confusion being established that harbors the ability to fully grasp the music knowledge, as well as to progress as a musician.

Music theory forms the foundation of learning to read, understanding and writing music. Once you have established a baseline with the ability to read music, you will be one step closer to playing scales, building chords, and being able to understand key signatures. When we look at this foundation, it primarily encompasses notes, rests, and beats. These basic elements are put together to establish a given rhythm, where the combination of these elements leads to reading, playing and studying music more effectively. As you progress through your musical training, you will start to manipulate and combine notes together into melodic and harmonic compound intervals. You will then be able to focus on establishing compound intervals on a melodic and harmonic scale.

Don't worry; by the end of this book, you will be well acquainted with these terms, as well as be able to successfully link music notation to the positioning of keyboard and/or piano keys. As you start to become more acquainted with music and its notation, you will start to develop a hunger for more in-depth knowledge. Music theory allows you to analyze the ins and outs of music, how the notes are strung together, as well as the best approach towards learning and understanding notation and key signatures. It is because of this that reading music remains an absolute necessity. This is primarily because without being able to read music, the ability to learn songs, songwriting, as well as the foundation of understanding where common errors occur, becomes hindered. This is why it is an absolute necessity to learn the key notations and strategies to read the music notation effectively, accurately, and with minimal mistakes. Music establishes a form of communication that enables you to connect with your listeners - to tell a story. A sense of inspiration also accompanies learning the theory of music. There is a thrill and feeling of complete satisfaction when you are able to build your first song, as well as when you do the first complete playthrough of your favorite classical piece. Music brings people together - friends, family, and even strangers.

Many who want to start learning more about music, automatically have the notion that the task that lies ahead of them is a daunting one. This makes the thought of giving up a lot more favorable than one would think. However, many discount the effectiveness of images and diagrams in learning music. When you are able to link the text to an image, not only are you able to remember the concept better, you are also enabling yourself to establish diagrammatical links (whether it be through a circle or a flow chart) between concepts, further enhancing your own understanding. What one typically finds is that images have the potential to trigger emotions, which makes remembering a concept that much easier.

This book is going to use a combination of text and images in order to enhance the reader's understanding. This book will use a bottom-up approach that focuses on building that strong foundation before moving onto more difficult concepts. This book should be used as a resource, for those new to music as a consistent learning source, and for those experienced in music as more of a refresher. With that being said, this book's author, Tommy Swandili, is an experienced producer and musician who has already made a name for himself through the other music-based publications he has created on Amazon.

The benefits of using this book rather than typical text-heavy books, is that this book will explain concepts using basic English, eliminating the jargon that causes confusion, especially for new musicians. In this book you will learn the exact techniques and strategies needed to learn the keyboard and/or piano efficiently, saving you quite a bit of money on private lessons. By the time you reach the end of this book, you should be able to understand the core concepts of playing music, reading music, composing music, and even being able to write your own songs. The information in this book focuses on a practical and straightforward approach that will definitely help you become a better musician.

Since about 90% of the information that our brains process is visual, it only takes 13 milliseconds for an image to be successfully processed by the human brain. By looking at an image after reading text from the same subject, understanding and interpreting the information becomes easier and will help you establish a strong foundation on which to build your music knowledge.

This book will enrich your current understanding of music, as well as establish a yearning towards wanting to learn more. Now is the time for you to start on your music journey. If not now, when? You are capable of understanding the essence of what music has to offer; and who wouldn't like to be able to whip out a piece of sheet music and start playing their favorite songs? With this book, you can, and you will become an even better keyboard and/or piano player. Your journey towards music success starts here.

Chapter 1: Music Theory Fundamentals

A standard, modern piano has a row of 88 black and white keys. 52 of these keys are white, consisting of notes for the C major scale. 36 of the keys are black keys, raised above the white keys. Some keyboards and pianos come with 66, 72, or 88 keys, which are divided into octaves of eight keys each. These keys are typically described using the C major scale - taking the eight keys from C on one octave, up to another C scale on another octave. The typical manner in which a C major scale will be performed includes the sequential usage of the following keys: C, D, E, F, G, A, B, C.

Before we take a further look into how these notes are arranged, as well as what additions can occur, we will look at some definitions that are essential to understanding music. They are as follows:

- Sound: Musical sounds refer to a regular pattern of vibrations that enter into your ear from an external source (an instrument, song, or crashing sound). As this vibration reaches our ears, internal organs then detect a specific frequency of the vibrations, sending them to the brain to allow us to perceive them as the pitch of a musical tone.
- Pitch: Refers to a specific property of music that occurs based on the rapidity of the vibrations oscillating from the external source of sound. This means that a higher pitch will be defined as more frequently oscillating vibrations that are regular. The contrast is therefore true

for a lower pitch, where there are larger intervals present between each oscillation.
- Note: A note is typically that of a single musical sound. There are different types of notes that have differing lengths of sound production. These can be classified as a semiquaver, quaver, crotchet, minum or semibreve.
- Timbre: The augmentation of music's tone, also known as tone quality, is the perceived sound quality that is perceived when listening to a musical note.
- Tone: An arrangement of pitch, quality and strength that is presented as a heard sound. It is important to note that there are different types of tones that are synonymous with different types of music genres. This becomes a pivotal point in understanding a specific music genre, or alternatively when you write music for a specific genre.

The notes in music are placed on a 'staff.' The staff in music consists of five solid lines with four spaces. When we find a note on each of these lines, or sitting in a specific space, they will represent a different note. The notes A-G move up the staff alphabetically. When we look at the distance between two different musical notes, we can define this as a music interval. In order to better understand what an interval constitutes, it is a whole step and a half step. With a whole step, you are simply moving up one note, thus you are moving from a space between two lines of the staff, onto the line itself (the reverse is also true for this). An example of a whole step would be moving from a C to a D. A half step, on the other hand, is moving between sharps and flats of specific notes; an example of this would be moving from C to C#. Making reference to a piano and/or keyboard, a half step would be moving from a white key to a black key (and vice versa), whereas a whole step would be moving from a white key to another white key, or from a black key to another black key. Intervals are numbered according to the amount of notes that are jumped in order for your initial note to get to your final note. To put this into perspective, if we were to move from a C to an E it would be a third interval as there would have been three steps taken.

When looking at the concept of what a root note is, it is simply just the first note that is present in a chord or scale. This means that if we were to look at the C major scale, the root note would be that of C.

There are two different types of clefs that are pertinent to understanding music notation. These clefs are the treble clef and the bass clef. The treble clef is seen as an ornamental 'G' shape, and is typically present on the left side of the staff. The treble clef characteristically refers to the upper registers of music. This means that instruments that utilize the higher registers, much like that of the flute and saxophone, will primarily have a treble clef written on the sheet music. When we are learning about the bass clef, we are primarily referring to the lower registers of music, such as those that use a lower pitch. Examples of instruments that use a bass clef are the tuba or cello. When we refer the treble and the bass clef in terms of the piano and/or keyboard, both are included. This is primarily because of the higher and lower ranges that can be played on the piano and/or keyboard.

Music is primarily created by combining the concepts of rhythm, melody, and harmony. It should be noted that specific forms of music are characteristically focused on only one or two of these domains, rather than always including all three. An example of this is African drum music that focuses purely on the rhythmic domain. Referring to rhythm, it is the regular patterns of sounds or pitches, enabling us to differentiate between music and noise. Melody refers to the combination of pitch and rhythm. Collectively, these are referred to as the tune, voice, or line, primarily stipulated as the linear succession of musical tones, grouped together in order to allow us to hear a single entity or sound. Harmony then refers to the vertical element of music, where a different amount of notes are played simultaneously on one instrument, or on other instruments. Harmony is also termed 'chords' in music.

When we look at key signatures, they are typically present at the beginning of the first staff, and to the right of the clef. Key signatures remind us as musicians, whether to play the notes in a sharp or a flat. Some keys within the range of keys on the piano and/or keyboard have sharps and flats, which are depicted by the black keys. In some cases where the key signature is not present on at the beginning of the staff, the individual notes themselves will have either a sharp (#) or a flat (♭) signature attached to them. It is the sharp or flat that will inform you of what register the musical piece should be played in.

As we delve into more detailed aspects of music theory, you will start to learn some tricks and mnemonics that help us remember and understand music theory more effectively. Examples of these can be the comparison between the treble clef and the bass clef. The treble clef, which provides us with the higher registers of music, consists of varying note names for the lines and spaces of the staff. Starting on the bottom line of the staff with an E, the space above it would be the next note (F), followed by the next line being a G. Thus, we can break down what note fits onto the staff using the following mnemonics:

- Notes EGBDF: These notes represent those that fall on the line of the staff, starting from the bottom line. An easy mnemonic to remember here would be, 'Every Good Boy Does Fine'.

- Notes FACE: These notes represent the spaces between two lines. With the first space being that at the bottom between notes E and G, the note that will sit here is F. The ascending spaces from there will then follow the 'FACE' mnemonic, until no more spaces are bound by the lines of the staff.'

The treble clef, however, is different from the bass clef, not only in the way it looks, but also in the arrangement of the notes on the staff in order to cater to the lower registers. When we are approached with a bass clef, it is almost as if a lower note is present in the same place as that of the treble clef's higher registers. To explain this better, we shall utilize the following mnemonics:

- Notes GBDFA: These notes represent those that fall on the line of the staff, beginning from the bottom line. The mnemonic to remember here is, 'Good Boys Do Fine Always'. It is important to establish that the notes will increase in an ascending manner.
- Notes ACEG: These notes are present in the spaces between two lines. The first space is present at the bottom of the staff, between notes G and B. The note that will be found here is A. As the notes ascend in spaces, 'All Cows Eat Grass' is the mnemonic that should be followed.

Chapter 2: Scales, Modes and Keys

When we delve a bit deeper into the analysis of music theory, we are required to analyze scales next. A scale is seen as a set of musical notes that are ordered together on the basis of similar frequency (or pitch). There are two main ranges of scales, referring to those that contain an ascending pitch, and contrastingly, those that have a descending pitch. These are termed ascending scales and descending scales respectively.

When we are talking about a scale, musically, we refer to each note of the scale as a particular degree. Along with this degree, comes a specific name. These names allow us to accurately determine which part of a scale is being referred to, saving time and maximizing the performance of the musician. These degrees along with their related names are as follows:

- The first degree (i.e. first note of the scale) is called the 'tonic'.
- The second degree (i.e second note of the scale) is called the 'supertonic'.
- The third degree (i.e third note of the scale) is called the 'mediant'.
- The fourth degree (i.e. fourth note of the scale) is called the 'subdominant'.
- The fifth degree (i.e. fifth note of the scale) is called the 'dominant'.
- The sixth degree (i.e. sixth note of the scale) is called the 'submediant'.
- The seventh degree (i.e. seventh note of the scale) is called the 'leading note'.

At this point you may be asking where the eighth degree is, as an octave has eight notes. Well, the eighth degree of a scale signifies the movement towards a higher octave, directly relating to the tonic of the higher octave. Another manner in which this can be conceptualized is by understanding that there are seven notes between each octave, thus, there can only be up to seven degrees before a higher octave is reached.

There are quite a number of scales that are present within music theory. The good news is that you will not need to learn all the different types at the beginning of your music career. We will primarily be looking at the major, minor and chromatic scales. However, in order to provide you a more holistic view on music theory, there are some scales that are present based on the amount of notes played within the scale. These are classically referred to scales that have a specific amount of different pitch classes in them. For example, the chromatic scale (which will be discussed in more detail later on) consists of 12 notes present per octave. A few other examples of scales are as follows:

- Pentatonic scale: Consists of five notes per octave, primarily focused on being an anhemitonic form. What this means is that there are no semitones (half step) present. This form of scale is typically seen in folk music, as well as that of many forms of traditional Asian music.
- Hexatonic scale: Consists of six notes per octave and is commonly found in folk music that is found in Western areas.
- Heptatonic Scale: Consists of seven notes per octave, and is seen as being the most common scale in use within modern Western music.
- Octatonic scale: Consists of eight notes per octave and is specifically used in the sheet music of jazz, as well as classical music that is more associated with the modern era.

The Difference Between Major And Minor Scales

The most common scales that we will be using when we learn music notation are the major and minor scales. However, learning them as single entities will help you understand each subject with more ease. It is resoundingly more difficult when needing to incorporate both major and minor scales into your songwriting, as well as when reading music. In order to understand these scales effectively, it is important to reiterate that a semitone refers to a half step, and a tone refers to a whole step.

The Major Scale

The major scale is a very common form of scale that is widely used within the music domain. How we define a major scale, is primarily by the sequence of semitones and tones (i.e. half steps and whole steps) that are present. Remember that there will only be seven degrees within a scale, hence the major scale is only made up of seven notes, with the eighth note leading into the next scale. This can be very confusing at the beginning, so we recommend spending adequate time on solidifying this concept. Thus, a typical combination for that of a major scale would be Tone - Tone - Semitone - Tone - Tone - Tone - Semitone. If we were to alter this to fit the half steps and whole steps dynamic, the above would be Whole step - Whole step - Half step - Whole step - Whole step - Whole step - Half step.

This is seen as the common formula, where starting on any note will create a major scale.

Let's try and build some scales together in order to drive the point home. We will start off with the C major scale which typically consists of C, D, E, F, G, A, B, C. The C major scale can therefore be constructed using the following steps:

- The starting note for the C major scale is the C.
- From the C, one will then take a whole step (or move a tone) to D.
- Another whole step is then taken from the D to the E.
- Following the major scale formula, a half step is now taken from E to F.
- A whole step is then taken from F to G.
- A further whole step is taken in order to move from G to A.
- The last whole step for the C major scale will be from A to B.
- To end off the C major scale, the final half step is then taken, taking us from B and returning to C, but an octave higher.

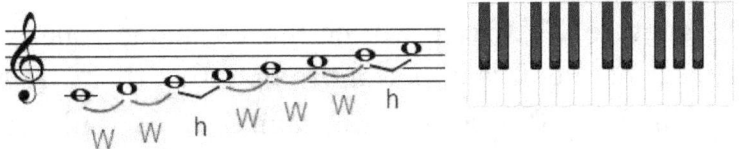

Let's take the creation of scales a bit further, as we focus on a scale that is different from your typical C major scale. We will do this in order to ascertain whether you have fully grasped the concepts of a major scale. The scale that we will learn now will be the D major scale. Note as you are going through this scale, that the D major scale consists of two sharp notes, with the primary notes featured in this scale being D, E, F#, G, A, B, C#, D. The building of this scale is as follows:

- Because we are dealing with the D major scale, the beginning note will be a D.
- The first whole step that will be taken will be from D to E.
- The second whole step in the major scale formula causes the movement from the E to F#.
- We then take a half step from the F# to G.
- Two subsequent whole steps will take us from G to A, and then from A to B.
- A whole step from B will result in a C#.
- Finally, to complete the D major scale, the final half step will return us to D, but an octave higher.

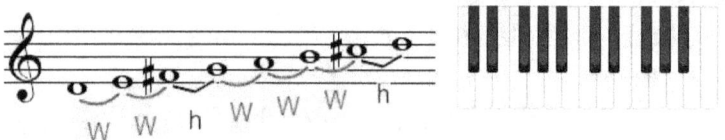

To ensure that the entire concept of a major scale is well understood, the final major scale that we will look at is one with a key signature. This scale will be the E♭ major scale. While building this scale, it is important to note that there are three flats in this scale (the E♭ is only counted once) and that the sequence of notes are E♭, F, G, A♭, B♭, C, D, E♭. The sequence followed to create this scale is as follows:

- The starting note of this scale will be E♭.
- A whole step is then taken to move from E♭ to F.
- The second whole step of the major scale is taken to move F to G.
- A half step then takes us from G to A♭.

- The subsequent three whole steps will then take us from A♭ to B♭, from B♭ to C, and from C to D, respectively.
- The final half step then moves from D to E♭, completing the E♭ major scale.

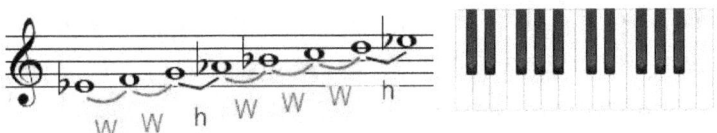

The Minor Scale

Minor scales can be seen as rather tricky, primarily because there are three types of minor scales, namely natural, melodic, and harmonic. Although we will be focusing on the harmonic minor scale, it is important to know information about the other minor scales should you be confronted with them when you are exploring through music. The differentiations between these three minor scales will be based on degree differences. With the natural minor scale, the third, sixth and seventh degrees need to be played at a half step (semitone) lower than what would originally have been present on a major scale. This completely eliminates the presence of any half steps, creating a scale that is completely whole steps. A melodic minor scale consists of a lowered third degree and a raised sixth degree, when compared to a major scale. When we look at the harmonic minor scale, it compares to the major scale by having a lowered third degree, a lowered sixth degree, and a seventh tone that is raised a half step.

A typical natural minor scale needs to be explained in order for the differing degrees to be well understood. When one makes a natural minor scale, the interval pattern that is used is Tone - Semitone - Tone - Tone - Semitone - Tone - Tone. This can also be read as Whole step - Half step - Whole step - Whole step - Half step - Whole step - Whole step.

The only difference with the formula for a natural minor scale, when converting it to a harmonic minor scale, would be the alteration of the seventh degree, raising it by a half step. Let's take a look at some natural minor scales, and then list how it can be changed into a harmonic minor scale. We will start off by constructing an A natural minor scale. An A natural minor scale has no notes with sharps or flats, with its primary sequence of notes being A, B, C, D, E, F, G, A. The method of construction is as follows:

- The natural A minor scale will start with an A.
- A whole step is then taken from A to B.
- A subsequent half step is then taken from B to C.
- Two whole steps are then taken from C to D, and then from D to E.
- The final half step then takes us from E to F.
- The final two whole steps will then take us from F to G, and from G back to A. However, the A will be the beginning (i.e. first degree) of the next octave.
- If we were to alter this into an A harmonic minor scale, the G will then be raised by a half step to A♭.

To create a visual contrast between the natural and harmonic minor scales. We will go through a C natural minor scale, establish the drawing thereof, and then compare it to the converted C harmonic minor scale so that you can visually see how the change in the seventh degree looks. The C natural minor scale consists of three flats, with its typical sequence being C, D, E♭, F, G, A♭, B♭. How this is constructed is as follows:

- The starting note for the C natural minor scale will be a C.
- A whole step is then taken to move from C to D.
- A half step then moves the D to an E♭.
- Two subsequent whole steps are taken to move the E♭ to a F, and the F to a G.
- The final half step then moves the G to an A♭.
- A whole step moves the A♭ to a B♭.
- The final then moves the B♭ to a C that exists as the first degree in another octave.

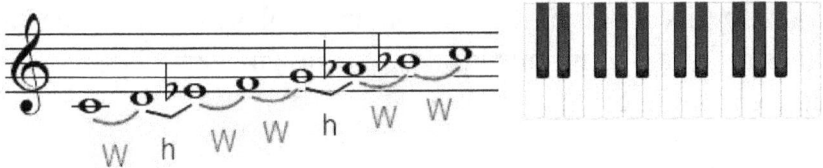

- A harmonic change is then made to the seventh degree (i.e. seventh note), raising it by a half step.
- The B♭ is then raised by a half step to B.
- The sequence of the C harmonic minor is then C, D, E♭, F, G, A♭, B.

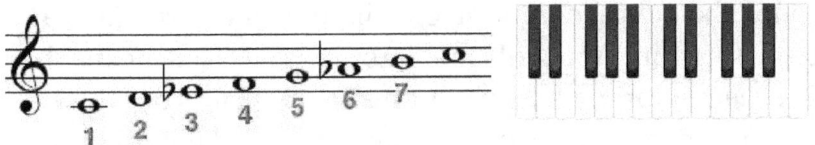

The Chromatic Scale

In comparison to the major and minor scales, the chromatic scale is very simple to understand. In music there are a total of 12 different notes. This scale focuses on all 12 notes present and is used primarily in Western music. What is unique about this scale is that the 12 notes are all semitones, and there are no tones present at all. In other words, the chromatic scale comprises completely out of half steps. A chromatic scale can therefore start at any of the 12 pitches. This means that if there was a chromatic scale that started on a C, by the end of the scale, a total of 12 different notes would have been played. These types of scales were widely used within the era of romantic music creation. Their utilization within the music construct domain can be used as transitional material, or to finalize a piece. Sometimes, chromatic scales are introduced as a glissando (a continuous upwards or downwards slide between two notes).

Modes

Modes are seen as a type of scale, whereby the alteration of a scale's notes results in the transition from a scale to that of a mode. The typical definition of a diatonic mode refers to a stepwise arrangement of a heptatonic scale. This means that the seven natural pitches (in terms of the scale's degrees) are able to form an octave without having altered the original established pattern. However, as soon as this primary pattern is altered, it begins to form a subclassification of the diatonic mode. There are seven main subclassifications of a diatonic mode. The classifications are the Ionian, Dorian, Phrygian, Lydian, Mixolydian, Aeolian and Locrian modes. Pay very close attention to the subtle differences present with the different modes as this will further allow you to grasp more complicated concepts in music later on.

Ionian Mode

An Ionian mode is seen as a very typical form of mode. It is classically represented by a natural diatonic scale that starts from C and ends on C. It can, thus, be related to a C major scale, with it being paramount that the beginning and end both are on a C. To create some sort of context as to where an Ionian mode can be found would be Vivaldi's Mandolin Concerto in C major, as well as Mozart's Flute and Harp Concerto in C major.

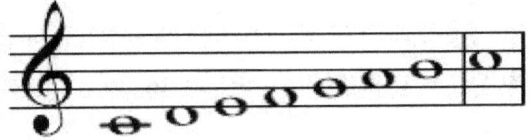

Dorian Mode

With the Dorian mode, it shows a very strong similarity with the natural minor scale. However, what sets this scale apart is the sixth degree. With a Dorian mode, the sixth degree is seen as a major sixth in comparison to the natural minor scale, which would have a minor sixth. The applications of a Dorian mode in the music industry include the song 'Billie Jean' that was sung by Michael Jackson, as well as 'Smoke on the Water' that was sung by Deep Purple.

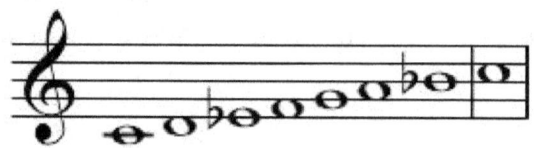

Phrygian Mode

The Phrygian mode is also similar to the natural minor scale, however, this difference is primarily on the second degree. It is on this note that a minor is present, not a major like that of which is present in the natural minor scale. With the Phrygian mode being the third type of mode, it is also known as the Spanish gypsy scale. The reason for this is due to the resemblance that it poses with the scales characteristically found in flamenco music. Musical pieces that include a Phrygian mode include Liszt's Hungarian Rhapsody No.2, along with Vaughan Williams's Fantasia on a Theme of Thoma Tallis.

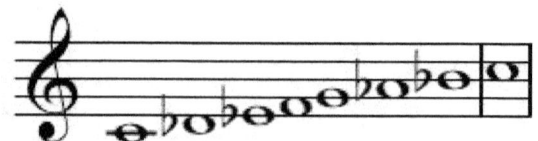

Lydian Mode

A Lydian mode is similar to the Ionian mode. The only difference is that in a Lydian mode, the fourth degree becomes a sharp, providing a rather unique, yet unsettling sound. The sounds created using a Lydian mode are characteristic. It has been employed in Chopin's Mazurka No.15 as well as Ludwig van Beethoven's String Quartet No.15 in A minor.

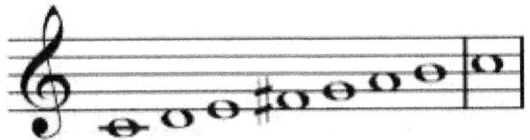

Mixolydian Mode

The comparison that is created with the Mixolydian mode is to that of the major scale. The differentiating factor between these two is the seventh degree, whereby the Mixolydian mode includes a flattened seventh degree compared to the major scale's seventh degree. The inclusions of this mode in the musical world include the song 'Norwegian Wood' sung by The Beatles, as well as the theme song to the television series, 'Star Trek.'

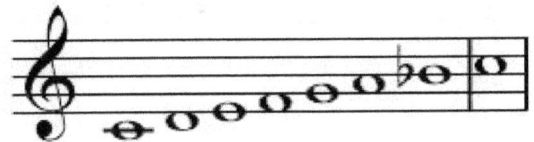

Aeolian Mode

The Aeolian mode is seen as a typical natural minor scale. There are absolutely no differences between the two, much like how the C to C major scale is directly related to the Ionian mode. The Aeolian mode is very common in songs, and not so much in classical music. Examples of the Aeolian mode are 'All along the Watchtower' sung by Bob Dylan, as well as 'Losing my Religion', by REM.

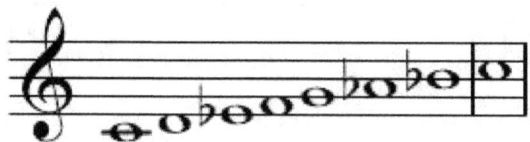

Locrian Mode

What makes the Locrian mode so unique is that it contains five notes in its scale that exhibit the flattened nature. These flattened notes are also present as a half step. This mode is present in the works of Rachmaninov, as well as in Sibelius's Symphony No.4 in A minor.

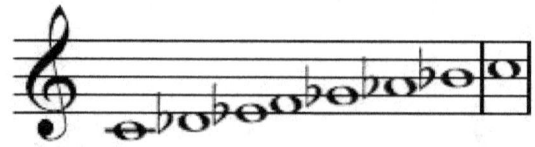

Keys

In music, there are quite a large amount of keys present. In this segment, we do not refer to keys as the physical keys that are present on the keyboard and/or piano; we are referring to a major, minor, or enharmonic key. The key is seen as the aspect around which the music revolves. Typically, the major key is based on a major scale. This means that a song played in the key of C major will be directly related to the seven notes that are present in the C major scale, the same way a song written in the key of F major will have its notes focused around the F major scale. A minor key is the complete opposite, whereby if we were to say that a song is played in the key of A♭, that it would follow the A♭ scale. Seeing as a minor scale has three categories, the same concept as above would be applied. An enharmonic key is seen as an identical key that is observed when one looks at both the sharp and flat key signatures. Primarily, it is when the enharmonic equivalent consists of the opposite key signature, thus, a specific sharp scale will have an enharmonic equivalent scale that exhibits a flat key signature. In order for you to understand this a bit better, we will provide some examples. Examples of enharmonic keys and their equivalents would be:

- A C# scale which has D♭ as its enharmonic equivalent.
- A D# scale which has E♭ as its enharmonic equivalent.
- A G# scale which has A♭ as its enharmonic equivalent.
- An A# scale which has B♭ as its enharmonic equivalent.

A very interesting key is that of the relative minor key. The reason this specific key is so interesting is that it exhibits the same key signature, but a different first degree (or tonic note). This is different to that of a parallel minor or major key, mainly because a parallel key would have the same first degree compared to that of the differing first degree in the relative minor key. Let us use some examples to solidify the concepts:

- A C♭ major scale will have an A♭ minor key as its relative minor equivalent.
- A G♭ major scale will have an E♭ minor key as its relative minor equivalent.
- A D♭ major scale will have a B♭ minor key as its relative minor equivalent.

The scales, modes, and keys that you have just learned may seem like a lot of information, and for someone just starting out as a musician, it genuinely is. However, this section has been simplified and fine tuned to such an extent that allows for ease of access, should you want to check your understanding as you progress through the rest of this book.

Chapter 3: Chords, Rhythms, And Movement In Music

Chords

As we start to delve deeper into music, we will learn about constructing chords. A chord is typically seen as the combination or layering of different notes and tones that are played at the same time. However, the manner in which these chords are built is dependent on the type of chord to be created. Typically, the components include a triad with that of a perfect fifth. Referring to that of a 'perfect fifth', it does not mean that one will only play a fifth degree, which is a common error that musicians make, especially when they are novice musicians. The perfect fifth refers to the combination of seven consecutive half steps. Thus, there are seven semitones in a perfect fifth. An example of a perfect fifth would be that from C to G. Taking the above into consideration, a major chord will consist of a major third and a perfect fifth; contrastingly, the minor chord will be made up of a minor third and a perfect fifth.

To understand the components of chords, we need to understand the different types of chords that exist. These are primarily dyads, triads, and tetrads. In music, especially for the piano and/or keyboard, a dyad is composed of two notes or pitches that are played simultaneously to create a chord. A typical example of a dyad would be playing C and E at the same time. There is usually an interval which is present with a dryad, as with what is present between C and E. This means that a dyad of C to E would suggest a key of C major, as it consists of two of the three notes that are typically present in a C major triad chord.

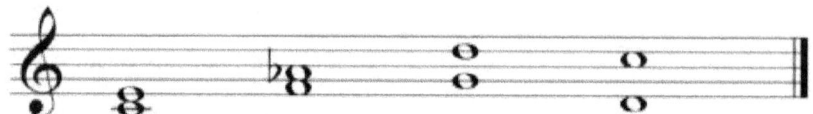

A triad is seen as the most common type of chord that is used in music. A triad consists of three notes. These three notes are typically the root note, the third degree, and the fifth degree. Simply put, these are the beginning note, the third note, and the fifth note, which are separated from each other by a third degree interval. This primarily means that each triad contains notes that are separated by a third degree interval (i.e. two notes between each triad component). In order to solidify this bit of knowledge, we can look at the C major triad. The C major triad consists of a C, E, and G. In these three notes, the C is the root note, E is seen as the third degree, with G being the fifth degree. Between the C and E, as well as the E and G, are two notes. This therefore depicts the separation of these notes using a third degree interval.

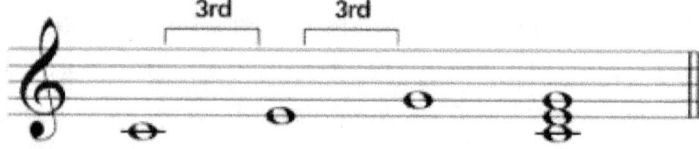

If we follow the above patterns, the amount of notes are present in a specific chord. There are four notes present in a tetrad. There are different types of tetrads in music, such as, seventh chords. However, that is some pretty advanced information which will be built on as your journey to becoming a musician progresses.

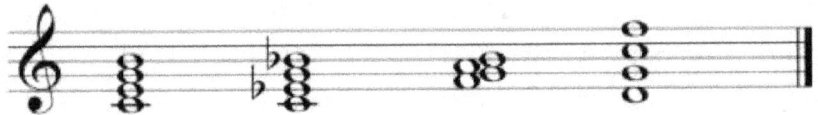

As we know, with scales, they can be composed of chords. This means that the type of chord you play will be dependent on the amount and presence of intervals that are between each note. It is this that we refer to as the quality of the chord. Furthermore, the quality of a chord will have a direct impact of how it sounds when played. Typically, what this can refer to is a direct tap into one's emotions. A major chord may sound rather happy, whereas when one plays a minor chord, they feel sad.

Now that you know about scales and what chords consist of, the next question you may have is how to construct chords when given a scale. This process is a simple one. You would start on the first note of the scale and move up in thirds, meaning that you would be skipping every alternate note. Placing this into musical talk, starting on the first degree, (also known as the root note) including the third and fifth degrees, will provide you with a three-note chord - known as a triad. The same would apply in terms of creating a dryad or tetrad, focusing on the amount of notes being played simultaneously, along with the amount of intervals present between each note. It is important to mention that more than one chord can be created from a single scale. An example of this would be a major scale, which gives rise to seven diatonic chords.

A fantastic manner in order to change registers, or to move notes or chords from one key to another, is to transpose the notes. A transposition is done by changing all the notes or chords from one major scale to another. One example could be a change from C major scale to a D major scale, where all the notes are changed by one whole step, acting as the primary distance between C and D. Looking at the following chord progression being C - F - A♭ - G - F - C, that is in the C major, if we were to transpose this into the key of D major, every note would be moved by one whole step. The result of this transposition would be D - G - B♭ - A - G - D.

Chord inversions can be rather difficult to understand. The primary way to understand this is to revise the regular position of a chord, along with what a root note is. If we are going to look at a C major triad, the normal positioning of the chord is with the root note being present at the bottom. In a triad, there is typically a first and second inversion that can take place. If the third degree of the chord (e.g. E in a C major triad) is at the bottom, this is called a first inversion. If we were to take the fifth degree and move it to the bottom, we would call this a second inversion.

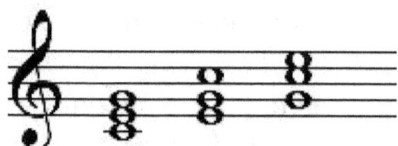

Some individuals, especially when songwriting, will have the option of changing the notes of a specific chord in a way that has the ability to alter the sound that is heard. This process is called 'Chord Voicing.' This means that if we were to voice an F major triad that is present in the root position, the notes can be arranged in any order as long as the F, A, and C are used in the F major scale, with F being the lowest note on the staff. It is noteworthy to mention that during the chord voicing process, one can move between the treble clef and the bass clef, transitioning between the upper and lower registers.

Chord progressions and arpeggios are the next step that we will be adding to your musician repertoire. A chord progression is seen as a series of two or more chords that are being used in the construction of music pieces. In order to show a progression, as well as the transposition between these chord progressions, roman numerals are used. Thus, using these roman numerals shows how a piece of music will unfold as it is being played. Arpeggios are typically a string of notes, consisting of any chord, whereby the notes are played one note at a time. This is in contrast to how notes are typically played, which is in a simultaneous manner. When we do the C major chord in an arpeggio format, it is playing each of those individual keys of the chord, one after each other.

Some chords just sound a lot better when played together, in comparison to others. It is a rule of thumb, that the first degree, fourth degree, and fifth degree notes of a chord will typically sound more pleasing than that of a second degree, third degree, and fifth degree chord. The chords which produce the most pleasing sounds stem from the C major, F major and G major scales. However, it's only when these sounds are played in a rhythmic manner, that they are pleasing to hear.

Rhythm

Rhythm is an important aspect to practice for any aspiring musician. Rhythm becomes important especially when you are playing in a band, or as a part of an orchestra. Having good rhythm enables you to stay in time with a band, allowing you to remain in beat with the rest of the procession. As you begin to start becoming acquainted with differing rhythms, you will develop sight-reading of good rhythms, as well as become able to play a variety of different rhythms by ear. However, this will take a lot of practice and experience to develop. When one understands rhythm, there is a decreased chance of either rushing the beat, or dragging the beat.

In order to understand rhythm, we need to analyze a few definitions and concepts. These are as follows:

- Beat: A beat is seen as a regular pulse that is repetitive in nature, along with a gap duration and speed which has the ability to allow us to count the beats, acknowledge accented musical sounds, as well as to map music towards a standard external beat regulator. An example of a beat regulator is a metronome.
- Bar: When we see vertical lines in the staff, it is indicative of bar lines. It is with this that we are able to group beats together. The manner in which we are able to assess the number of beats that are present in the bar is through the use of time signatures. There are typically three types of bar lines. A single bar line divides the beats, the double barline indicates the end of a section, with the final bar line indicating the end of the music piece.
- Time signatures: A time signature is seen as a part of musical notation that denotes the type of beat, the amount of beats that are present, as well as the number of beats that are present in a bar. Characteristically, one would find the presence of a time signature in the very

first bar, after the double bar line. Time signatures are typically given by four beats in a bar. A duplet is when there are two beats in a bar, a triple is when there are three beats in a bar, with a quadruple being a four beat count in a bar.

- Tempo: When we alter the speed of the beats, we are changing the tempo of the piece. The manner in which we increase or decrease tempo is by changing the amount of beats that occur per minute. One can further change the note value to have an effect on the tempo. If one were to change crotchets to minims, the music would be performed at half of its original tempo.

The time signatures are further divided into two main categories, simple and complex. With simple time signatures, there is a single regular beat that is equal to one regular beat count. This means that if one were to see a 4/4 time signature, it would denote four beats taking place within the bar. A 2/4 and a 3/4 would then denote a duplet and triple respectfully. With a compound time signature, it is the incorporation of three beats equal to one regular beat count. Thus, a full simple time signature would be 4/4 , and a compound time signature would either be 6/8, 9/8, or 12/8.

It is now time to pull all of the concepts that you have already learned into creating your own rhythm. Here are a few steps that you can include in order to successfully create your own first rhythm:

- It is important to find a tempo that you feel comfortable with. How musicians tend to come up with their tempo, is by counting out loud. Counting to four would produce a four-beat cycle, establishing s simple time signature.

- When you are able to find your original tempo, you can play around with doubling and quadrupling of the notes to find a repetitive note cycle that you enjoy.
- You can add onto your rhythm manipulation by accenting subdivisions of your rhythm. This adds a sense of uniqueness to your rhythmic creation.
- Chord voicing along with inversions may provide a very distinct yet pleasurable feel to your rhythm, which can be explored in a variety of different ways.

Movement in Music

Timbre and tone are important aspects that enable one to really flourish when doing movement pieces in tandem with music. When we use the timbre to augment the tone's quality, we are able to implement more brisk movements that are more profound, within a specific tone. When we are able to arrange our sounds based on their pitch, quality and strength, we are able to find specific movements and movement styles that complement the sounds and music composed.

When we combine sounds together, they can either result in a consonance or dissonance. A consonant musical sound is typically described as being pleasant and soothing. Thus, sounds which are described as being comfortable, will be classified as being in consonance. Dissonance is when a musical sound is categorized as sharp, unsettling or unnerving, establishing a sense of tension when being heard. When we watch romantic movies, we are more likely to hear consonant sounds, whereby a thriller or horror movie is more likely to have dissonant sounds.

Referring to drama, it is seen as the use of music and sound to express emotions with the aid of action. The effectiveness of a dramatic performance is based on the strength of the bond between movement and sound, establishing a setting that invigorates audiences while allowing the sounds to be heard effectively.

Chapter 4: Songwriting

Songwriting is not as simple as some would think. It requires revision after revision, the scrapping of ideas, and ensuring that the words match the sounds. It is also noteworthy to mention that there is no fixed manner to write a song. There are different routes and methods that may suit some individuals better than others. When you are about to start writing a song, it is always valuable to do some introspection. What is the message or story that you want to tell? This is where you start finding the melody and rhythm that will not only bring your story to life, but allow you to tell this story to your listeners in a way that is clear and easy to understand. Some songwriters find that they enjoy scripting the chorus first, and then finding a story to complement it.

It helps to write about what you know or something that is important to you. It is a lot easier to write about a subject you are passionate about, or a real-life story that happened to you. Try to have a universal message that listeners can relate to. When you are able to bring out the emotion of a song, you are enabling the listeners to feel your raw emotions, and to understand the journey you had in creating this song. It is important to be passionate about your songwriting. Whilst you are constructing your lyrics, you need to ask yourself whether or not you are delivering your desired message through the melody and lyrics that you have chosen.

How do we go about creating a melody that matches our lyrics? When you start creating your melody, start off by choosing a scale. The reason you should start with a scale is that it limits the amount of notes you can plot, ensuring that you don't waste time looking for notes by ear or checking random keys on your piano and/or keyboards to see if one works. Many decide to use a C major pentatonic scale, which contains C, D, E, G and A. Next, focus on creating a rhythmic succession of the notes in your scale, establishing a contour that establishes how your melody will rise, fall, or remain constant. Once you have the melody, you can play around with the sounds you want to hear. This is important as they need to complement each other. Once you have these components, it is time to revisit your contour line, change some notes around if necessary, and start to fill in your sheet music. If you feel that something is out of place, fix it, whether it be adding extra notes, removing notes, or adjusting the length of these notes.

It is important to also know which genre in which you will be writing your song. As we tackle different genres, it is important that we know what type of audience we want to reach, adapting the genre we write in order to reach them effectively. Some of the different genres used in songwriting include pop, country, rock, urban and blues, amongst many others. The selection of the genre is a very important step as some listeners will prefer to listen to specific genres, while completely avoiding others. If you are planning on writing music and songs for a publisher, your genre is pivotal, as it is one of the core criteria, off of which they will base your music.

It is important to understand that your first song is not going to be perfect. The same may be relevant for your one hundredth song. Songwriting is a skill, one that you will become better at the more you practice. Remember, songwriting, much like with writing music, takes revisiting concepts in order to solidify your knowledge. Music is all about trying until you succeed, and using your failures as stepping stones on your journey in becoming the best musician you can be.

Chapter 5: Orders and Circles

Orders and circles significantly add to your musical knowledge. Focusing on orders, we analyze the order of flats and the order of sharps. These are typically the sequence of flats and sharps as they move along scales and the staff. Sharps will typically follow an ascending pattern from F to B, whereas the flats will typically move in the opposite direction of sharps, primarily from B to F.

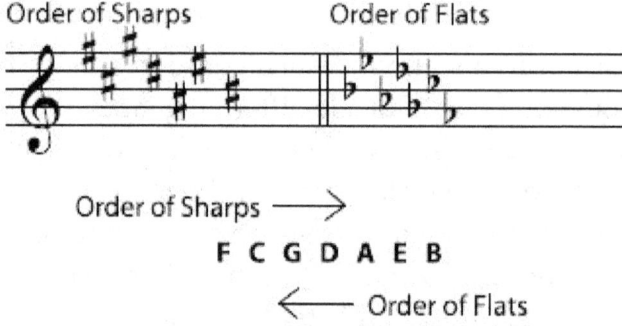

The circles of fourths and fifths are primarily present to show the relationship between the 12 notes in music. When we look at the circle of fourths, they primarily let you know how many flats there are in each key. Thus, the circle of fourths will move counterclockwise from C major (which correlates with the twelfth hour on a clock). The purpose of the circle of fourths is primarily to learn which notes will turn into flats. The circle of fifths moves from C major in the clockwise direction, letting us know which notes will turn into sharps, as well as the amount of sharps present. When looking at the circle, one will be able to see that a G major scale has one sharp, whereas the contrasting F major has one flat. However, what people have done is combine the circle of fourths and fifths together into one circle, terming it the circle of fifths. The reason that the circle is termed the circle of fifths is because the key signature is separated by the distance that correlates with a fifth interval. When we start at C major (correlating with the 12th hour on a clock), and move five whole steps up, and add a sharp in the process, the proper amount of sharps for that key are identified.

One needs to become familiar with the order in which we add sharps. This order is F, C, G, D, A, E, B - correlating with the sequence explained above. So when we analyze the key of C, we can see that there are no sharps present. When we take those five steps up, we reach G. In the key of G, we see that there is one sharp present, which has to be an F# based on the order of sharp addition. Therefore, every single time that one moves five steps up, you will add another sharp. This is where the circle of fifths correlates with the movement of five whole steps between major scales.

The circle of fourths, as previously mentioned, tells us the flats that are present in keys. However, the steps are four up instead of five, correlating with the circle of fourths. Starting from C, there are no flats present. However, when we take those first four whole steps up, we reach an F that the circle shows has one flat. If we were to follow the sequence in which we add flats, which is B, E, A, D, G, C, F, we would be able to identify that a F major scale will consist of a B flat. This means that every time one takes four steps up, another flat is added.

It is important to remember that moving left from the C position gives you the degrees of flats present (referring to the circle of fourths), whereas moving right from the C position will give you the degrees of sharps that are present (referring to the circle of fifths).

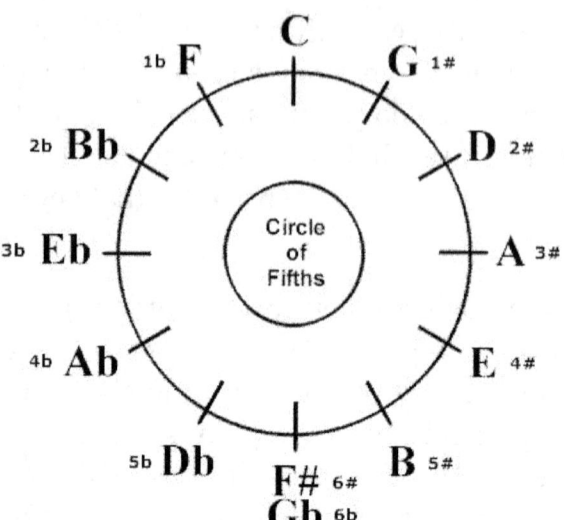

Conclusion

The strategies that have been covered in this book have allowed you to grasp the concepts that one would typically pay lots of money for in private instruction. We have paved the journey of learning how to play music, read music, write songs, as well as compose your own melodies, chords, and musical pieces to enhance dramatic performances. It is intended to provide a firm grasp on both the text and visual aspects in this book, where we included significant images that are meant to enhance your understanding of the content.

The exact techniques of learning music, as well as its fundamentals, have been placed in a streamlined fashion that allows you to revisit the basics if you ever feel the need to. In this book, we further focused on how to read music, what sheet music looks like, as well as what the different forms of notation mean. We looked at the definitions of pitch, sound, note, timbre and tone, relating them to the concepts of an octave, harmony, melody and rhythm. We even went further to differentiate between the different clefs that are found in music, as well as what this means for their respective note arrangements on the staff.

You were then introduced to scales, their different types, as well as how modes and keys relate to each other in the creation of song. Building on the idea of songwriting, tricks and tips were given to you to enhance your understanding, as well as guide you to where the best place to start writing a song would be. The creation of these songs were then supplemented with the information that was explained about chords, rhythms, and how to link movement to music.

Lastly, we tackled one of the most confusing aspects in music, the circles of fourths and fifths. We found an easy way to read them, what one actually means when they mean the circle of fourths (i.e. the presence of flats anti-clockwise from C), as well as when one refers to the circle of fifths (i.e. the presence of sharps clockwise from C).

Music on its own is difficult to learn, especially when you have no idea where you should start. However, this book has provided you with a simple guide that is informative, accurate, and easy to understand. You must remember that becoming a musician doesn't happen overnight. It requires constant reevaluation of one's skills, knowledge and experience, focusing on the gaps that you don't know and establishing ways to fill these gaps.

You now have the knowledge about key notations and strategies that will enable you to read music with ease. Remember, music establishes a form of communication that enables you to connect with your listeners, as well as other musicians. It is an art that allows you to tell your story in the manner that you see best. We hope that having reached the end of this book, you are left inspired and want to continue learning other aspects of music theory. You now have the thrill, feeling of satisfaction, and confidence in being able to write your first song. Music brings people together, whether it be friends, family, or strangers. It is a worldwide language that couples with personal growth as you start to build your own repertoire of musical skill. You have now learned the basics of what there is to know about musical theory regarding the piano and/or keyboard. There is still so much waiting for you on the path of becoming the best musician you can be.

Discover "How to Find Your Sound"

http://musicprod.ontrapages.com/

Swindali music coaching/Skype lessons.

Email djswindali@gmail.com for info and pricing

References

Alexis, C. (2018, November 12). *29 incredible stats that prove the power of visual marketing.* MovableInk. https://movableink.com/blog/29-incredible-stats-that-prove-the-power-of-visual-marketing/

Farrant, D. (2019). *Types of musical scales: A beginner's guide.* Hello Music Theory: Learn Music Theory Online. https://hellomusictheory.com/learn/music-scales-beginners-guide/

Frederick, R. (n.d.). *TIP #5: Write your song in a genre.* Songwriting Tips and Inspiration. https://robinfrederick.com/five-essential-songwriting-tips/tip-5-write-your-song-in-a-genre/#:~:text=Songwriting%2C%20too%2C%20comes%20in%20different

Gateway, M. (2019, August 22). *Music interval - Music theory 101.* Music Gateway. https://www.musicgateway.com/blog/how-to/music-intervals-theory-with-reference-songs

Gutierrez, K. (2019). *Studies confirm the power of visuals in eLearning.* Shiftelearning.Com. https://www.shiftelearning.com/blog/bid/350326/studies-confirm-the-power-of-visuals-in-elearning

Johnson, C. (2019, August 22). *What is rhythm & why is it so important.* Music Gateway. https://www.musicgateway.com/blog/how-to/what-is-rhythm-why-is-it-so-important#:~:text=Importance%20of%20Having%20G ood%20Rhythm&text=Having%20a%20good%20rhythm%20enables

Pilhofer, M. (2016). *What is music theory? - Dummies.* Dummies. https://www.dummies.com/art-center/music/what-is-music-theory/

Pouska, A. (2019). *Keys in music | Harmony.* StudyBass. https://www.studybass.com/lessons/harmony/keys-in-music/

Ross, J. (2019, May 4). *How many musical scales are there (the complete guide).* Joshua Ross. https://joshuarosspiano.com/how-many-musical-scales-are-there/

Team, M. U. (2017, February 14). *Consonance & dissonance in music.* Musical U. https://www.musical-u.com/learn/consonance-dissonance-music/

Team, M. U. (2017, November 30). *About finding chords in scales.* Musical U. https://www.musical-u.com/learn/about-finding-chords-in-scales/#

Team, M. U. (2018, June 12). *Exploring common chord progressions.* Musical U. https://www.musical-u.com/learn/exploring-common-chord-progressions/

Writer, M. C. (2019, October 1). *Tips for beginning songwriters | Songwriting tips.* Music City SongStar. https://musiccitysongstar.com/songwriting-tips-for-beginners/

All images were created using music composition software, primarily Notation, Composer and Canorus. The word edits were then made using Goodnotes on the iPad.

www.ingramcontent.com/pod-product-compliance
Lightning Source LLC
Chambersburg PA
CBHW071547080526
44588CB00011B/1824